W9-AOS-036

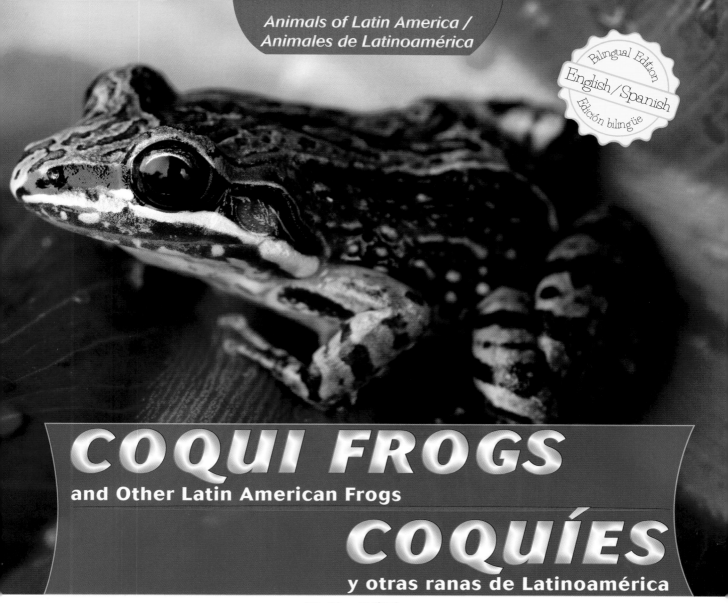

Animals of Latin America /
Animales de Latinoamérica

Bilingual Edition
English / Spanish
Edición bilingüe

COQUI FROGS
and Other Latin American Frogs

COQUÍES
y otras ranas de Latinoamérica

Zella Williams
Traducción al español: Ma. Pilar Obregón

PowerKiDS press. & **Editorial Buenas Letras**™
New York

Published in 2010 by The Rosen Publishing Group, Inc.
29 East 21st Street, New York, NY 10010

Copyright © 2010 by The Rosen Publishing Group, Inc.

All rights reserved. No part of this book may be reproduced in any form without permission in writing from the publisher, except by a reviewer.

First Edition

Editor: Joanne Randolph
Book Design: Kate Laczynski
Photo Researcher: Jessica Gerweck

Photo Credits: Cover, pp. 1, 5, 9 (inset), 17 Shutterstock.com; pp. 7, 11 © Kevin Schafer/Corbis; p. 9 © Stephanie Maze/Corbis; p. 13 © Michael & Patricia Fogden/Corbis; p. 15 © Dante Fenolio/Photo Researchers, Inc.; p. 19 Ken Lucas/Getty Images; p. 21 Gail Shumway/Getty Images.

Library of Congress Cataloging-in-Publication Data

Williams, Zella.
  Coqui frogs and other Latin American frogs /Coquíes y otras ranas de Latinoamérica / Zella Williams. — 1st ed.
     p. cm. — (Animals of Latin America = Animales de Latinoamérica)
  Includes index.
  ISBN 978-1-4042-8148-6 (library binding) — ISBN 978-1-4358-3382-1 (pbk.) —
  ISBN 978-1-4358-3383-8 (6-pack)
  1. Eleutherodactylus coqui—Latin America—Juvenile literature. 2. Frogs—Latin America—Juvenile literature. I. Title.
  QL668.E257W55 2010
  597.87'54098—dc22
                              2009006287

Manufactured in the United States of America

Contents

R0431198416

Contenido

The calls of the coqui frog ring out through the night. Ko-kee! Ko-kee! The sound this noisy frog makes gave it its name. The small, grayish brown coqui frog is **native** to Puerto Rico, but it lives in many places throughout the Caribbean Islands and even in Louisiana, Hawaii, and parts of Central America and South America.

El canto de la rana coquí se escucha por las noches. ¡Co-quí! ¡Co-quí! El canto le da el nombre a esta pequeña rana de color castaño-grisáceo. El coquí es **nativo** de Puerto Rico, pero vive en muchos lugares, desde las islas del Caribe, hasta Luisiana, Hawai y partes de Centro y Sudamérica.

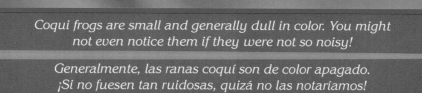

Coqui frogs are small and generally dull in color. You might
not even notice them if they were not so noisy!

*Generalmente, las ranas coquí son de color apagado.
¡Si no fuesen tan ruidosas, quizá no las notaríamos!*

5

There are 17 different species, or kinds, of coquis in Puerto Rico. Scientists guess that there are 20,000 frogs in 2.5 acres (1 ha) of land there. That is a lot of frogs! The frog is so common that it has become an **unofficial** national **symbol**. Puerto Ricans have written many stories, poems, and songs about their beloved coqui.

En Puerto Rico existen 17 especies, o tipos, distintos de coquíes. Los investigadores creen que en Puerto Rico hay 20,000 ranas en 2.5 acres (1 ha) de tierra. ¡Eso es muchísimas ranas! Hay tantas coquíes en Puerto Rico que se han convertido en el **símbolo no oficial** de la isla. Los puertorriqueños han escrito muchas historias, poemas y canciones sobre su querida rana coquí.

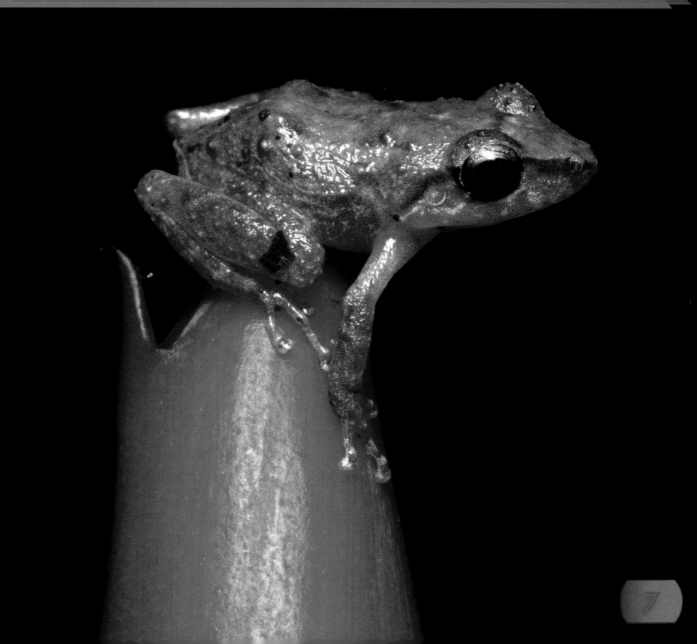

Male coquis are the only ones that sing. They start their song
when the Sun goes down and keep singing until dawn.

Sólo las coquíes macho cantan. Estas ranas comienzan a cantar al caer el sol
y siguen cantando hasta el amanecer.

The coqui has played a part in Puerto Rican life for a very long time. **Ancient** cave paintings and art of the Taíno Indians often show the frog. There are many Taíno stories about the coqui, too. In one of them, the god Juracán kills a wise prince, named Coquí. The god Yuquiyú makes the coqui frog so people will remember the prince.

El coquí ha sido parte de la vida de Puerto Rico durante mucho tiempo. Con frecuencia, las ranas aparecen en las antiguas pinturas de cuevas de los indios taíno. Además, hay muchas historias de los taínos en los que se habla de las ranas. En una de ellas, el dios Juracán mata a un príncipe muy sabio, llamado Coquí. Se dice que el dios Yuquiyú creó la rana coquí para que la gente recordara al príncipe.

The Taíno left paintings, such as these, on rocks in Puerto Rico, some of which showed the coqui. Inset: Coquis have lived in Puerto Rico for thousands of years.

Los Taíno dejaron pinturas, como éstas, en las rocas de Puerto Rico. En muchas se mostraba al coquí. Recuadro: El coquí ha vivido en Puerto Rico durante miles de años.

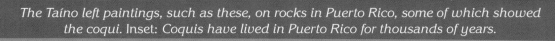

9

Coqui frogs can live almost anywhere that is wet for much of the year. This makes Caribbean rain forests a great home for these tree frogs. They sit high up in the rain forest trees for most of the night. Then they drop down to the ground and hide for the day.

Las ranas coquí pueden vivir la mayor parte del año en cualquier zona húmeda. Es por eso que la selva tropical del Caribe es un gran hogar para estas ranas. Durante la noche, las ranas se suben a la copa de los árboles. Durante el día, bajan al suelo y se esconden.

Coqui frogs have sticky toe pads, which help them stick to leaves and trees.
These frogs grow to be about 1.3 to 1.6 inches (3–4 cm) long.

Las ranas coquí tienen patas pegajosas que les ayudan a trepar a las hojas de los árboles.
Las coquíes llegan a medir de 1.3 a 1.6 pulgadas (3–4 cm) de largo.

11

Coquis play a big part in Puerto Rico's **ecosystem**. They eat a huge number of arthropods, such as roaches, crickets, spiders, and ants. In turn, coquis are food to snakes, birds, and large crab spiders. Their dull coloring and small size help hide them, but many coquis end up as lunch. Coquis come together and make babies throughout the year. The female lays about 28 eggs and then the male guards them.

Los coquíes juegan un papel importante en el **ecosistema** de Puerto Rico. Estas ranas comen muchos artrópodos, como cucarachas, grillos, y hormigas. A su vez, los coquíes son alimento para las serpientes, aves y grandes arañas. Aunque su color apagado les ayuda a esconderse, muchas ranas terminan siendo el almuerzo de otros animales. Los coquíes tienen crías todo el año. Las hembras ponen unos 28 huevos y el macho se encarga de cuidarlos.

Coqui frogs' eggs do not need to be laid in water, as many other frogs' eggs do.
This lets coquis live in more different kinds of places than other frogs can.

Los huevos de los coquíes no tienen que ponerse en agua, como sucede con otros tipos de ranas.
Esto permite que los coquíes vivan en lugares diferentes a otras ranas.

13

The coqui is in danger in Puerto Rico, where some kinds of coquis are disappearing. Yet this tiny frog is considered a pest in Hawaii, where it is taking over. Hawaii has no native frogs, and people are not used to the coquis' singing. The noise bothers Hawaiians, but this is not the biggest problem. The frog is harming Hawaii's ecosystem.

En Puerto Rico, algunas clases de coquíes están en peligro de desaparecer. Mientras tanto, en Hawai, se les considera una peste que está acabando con el medioambiente. Hawai no tiene ranas nativas, y las personas no están acostumbradas a su canto. El canto molesta a muchos hawaianos. Pero éste no es el problema principal.
El verdadero problema es que los coquíes están dañando el ecosistema de Hawai.

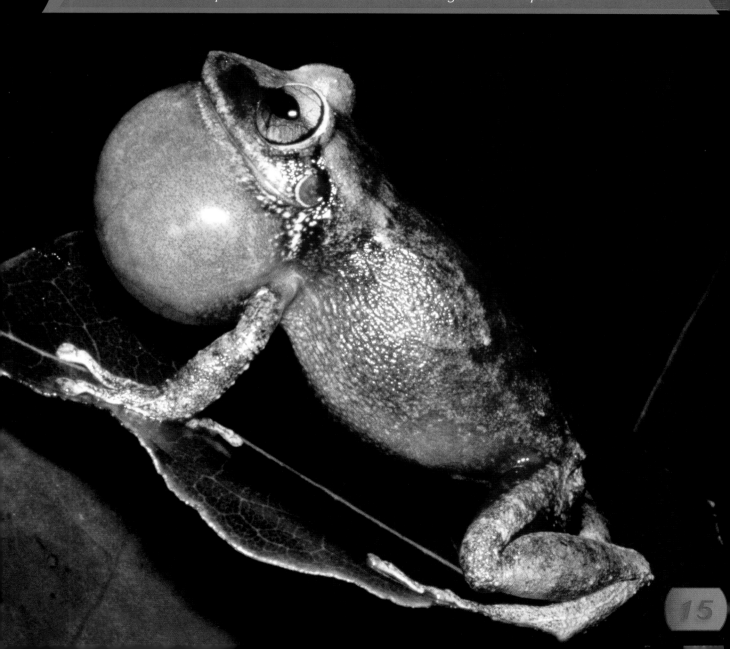

This coqui puffs up its throat to make its call. A group of frogs singing together can make a sound that is about as loud as a lawn mower.

Este coquí infla su garganta antes de cantar. Un grupo de ranas cantando pueden hacer tanto ruido como una segadora de césped.

15

Coqui frogs are dull in color and only their voices let people know they are there. The **poison** dart frog, on the other hand, is flashier than the coqui. This brightly colored frog lives in the rain forests of Latin America. The poison dart frog can be yellow, gold, red, green, blue, or black.

Las ranas coquí son de color opaco y pueden cantar para avisar dónde se encuentran. Por su parte, la rana dardo **venenoso**, es muy brillante. Esta rana de colores brillantes vive en la selva tropical de Latinoamérica. La rana dardo venenoso puede ser amarilla, dorada, roja, verde, azul o blanca.

Poison dart frogs can be beautiful with their brightly colored skin.
This is a red-backed poison dart frog.

Las ranas dardo venenoso pueden ser muy bellas gracias a su piel de colores brillantes.
Esta rana dardo tiene el lomo de color rojo.

17

The poison dart frog's bold coloring is a warning. It lets animals know that the frog is poisonous if eaten. The Emberá Choco people of Colombia have long used the poison from the golden poison dart frog to help them hunt. They use the poison to coat their blowgun darts.

El color de la rana dardo es una advertencia. Así les avisan a otros animales que no las coman porque son venenosas. Los indígenas colombianos emberá choco han usado a las ranas dardo durante años en sus cacerías. Los emberá choco usan el veneno en los dardos que lanzan con unos tubos largos y angostos llamados cerbatanas.

The golden poison dart frog is one of the deadliest animals on Earth. The poison in its skin can kill up to 10 full-grown men.

La rana dardo dorada es uno de los animales más venenosos del mundo. El veneno de su piel puede matar a 10 personas adultas.

The red-eyed tree frog lives in the rain forests of southern Mexico, Central America, and northern South America. It hunts at night and almost never leaves the trees. Both the coqui and the red-eyed tree frog have sticky pads on their toes. These pads let the frogs climb trees and leaves.

Las ranas de ojos rojos viven en las selvas tropicales del sur de México, en Centroamérica y el norte de Sudamérica. Las ranas de ojos rojos cazan de noche y casi nunca dejan los árboles. Al igual que las coquíes, las ranas de ojos rojos tienen patas pegajosas. Estas patas son una buena ayuda para trepar en los árboles.

The red-eyed tree frog is about 1.5 to 2.75 inches (4–7 cm) long.

La rana de ojos rojos mide entre 1.75 y 2.75 pulgadas (4–7 cm) de largo.

21

Frogs, from noisy coquis to colorful poison dart frogs, are important. Frogs eat bugs that may spread illness and they feed many animals. Many Latin American frogs are being studied for their possible use in medicine. Many frogs are disappearing, though. We must do what we can to keep these frogs singing.

Las ranas, como las coquíes y las dardo son muy importantes. Las ranas comen muchos insectos que pueden transmitir enfermedades. Además, son el alimento de muchos animales. Muchas ranas de Latinoamérica están siendo estudiadas para usarlas en la medicina. El problema es que muchas ranas están desapareciendo. Debemos hacer todo lo posible para mantener a estas ranas cantando por muchos años más.

Glossary

ancient (AYN-shent) Very old, from a long time ago.

ecosystem (EE-koh-sis-tem) A community of living things and the place in which they live.

native (NAY-tiv) Born or grown in a certain place or country.

poison (POY-zun) Matter made by an animal's body that causes pain or death.

symbol (SIM-bul) Something that stands for something else.

unofficial (un-uh-FIH-shul) Generally believed but not formally or legally recognized.

Glosario

antiguo Viejo. De hace mucho tiempo.

ecosistema (el) Una comunidad de organismos vivos y el lugar en el que viven.

nativo, va Nacido en un cierto lugar o país.

no oficial Algo que se considera oficial pero no es reconocido formalmente.

símbolo (el) Un objeto o pintura que representa algo distinto.

veneno (el) Substancia de ciertos animales que puede causar dolor o muerte.

Index

Índice

Web Sites / Páginas de Internet

Due to the changing nature of Internet links, PowerKids Press and Editorial Buenas Letras have developed an online list of Web sites related to the subject of this book. This site is updated regularly. Please use this link to access the list:
www.powerkidslinks.com/anla/coqui/